KENTUCKY

KENTUCKY

HISTORIC HOUSES
AND HORSE FARMS OF
BLUEGRASS COUNTRY

PHOTOGRAPHS BY

PIETER ESTERSOHN

INTRODUCTION BY

W. GAY READING

THE MONACELLI PRESS

Copyright © 2014 The Monacelli Press

Photographs © 2014 Pieter Estersohn

Published in the United States by
The Monacelli Press

All rights reserved

Library of Congress Control Number 2013955484

ISBN 978-158093-3568

Design: Patrick Seymour and Catarina Tsang,
Tsang Seymour

Printed in China

www.monacellipress.com

The Monacelli Press acknowledges, with thanks, the editorial contributions of James Birchfield, Michele Keith, Mikhaela Mahony, Marty Perry, Gay Reading, Julia Reed, and David Stuart in the compilation of this book.

CONTENTS

INTRODUCTION
12

ASHLAND
LEXINGTON
16

SIMPSON FARM
PARIS
32

WELCOME HALL
VERSAILLES
46

BOTHERUM
LEXINGTON
60

SHAKER VILLAGE
PLEASANT HILL
72

WARD HALL
GEORGETOWN
86

MAPLE HILL
C. V. WHITNEY FARM
LEXINGTON
102

WAVELAND
LEXINGTON
116

ELLEY VILLA
LEXINGTON
134

WARWICK
HARRODSBURG
148

LIBERTY HALL
FRANKFORT
158

POPE VILLA
LEXINGTON
174

WALNUT HALL
LEXINGTON
186

OVERBROOK FARM
LEXINGTON
196

ALEXANDER MOORE HOUSE
LEXINGTON
210

JANUARY HOUSE
LEXINGTON
220

GAINESWAY FARM
LEXINGTON
232

IROQUOIS HUNT CLUB
LEXINGTON
248

INTRODUCTION

It is a good thing when one is asked to preface a work such as this and thus must evaluate the enduring nature of the place he calls home and loves. That the request is prompted by the creation of images evocative of that love makes the experience all the better. I do believe that Pieter Estersohn's images of the Bluegrass Country should first of all be considered as a collection of photographs of very high artistic merit. Here we see Estersohn as a connoisseur of light and form. There is art also in the relationship between the images selected and a direct correlation with the artist's personal interest in historic houses. His visits to the Bluegrass prompted him to undertake the work, and we who have been here for a long time appreciate that he finds beauty in our heritage. His is a democratic approach. It is a portrait with "warts and all," something our down-to-earth ancestors often demanded in images of themselves and their loved ones. But the subjects are not mundane; there is a good reason for their likenesses to be taken. By considering houses and farms together, Estersohn is acknowledging what makes the Bluegrass exceptional, the land itself.

My own interest and fond attachment to central Kentucky is in part attributable to my direct relationship with one Colonel George Reading (1725-1792), soldier, landholder, and probably surveyor. A native of New Jersey, he wrote in July 1779 from western Pennsylvania, where he served in the American Revolution, "I propose sending [son] John down to Kentucky and the falls of Ohio, in a month or six weeks to take up and secure land, if he likes the country. We have the most favorable accounts of that country. It is a land to be desired, where the winter (not like Pharoah's lean kine) dont devour the summer; withal very healthy, where I hope to end my days." He came to Bourbon County, Virginia, in 1780. By 1783 he could write,

"We have all things in plenty, and live as well as any person in Kentucky." What he had the most of was land, his other wants seeming to be few. When Col. George died, in the year Kentucky became a State (actually one of the Commonwealths in our nation) he left his son John a parcel of Kentucky land surveyed by frontiersman Simon Kenton along with other lands to be held in common with his brothers. I cite this Kentucky pioneer to point out that it is the quality of the land that has always been the proper attraction to this place.

The Reading family entered Kentucky by way of the Ohio River. Modern highways still follow the tracks worn into the land from that river to the fertile center by long-gone herds of animals and used by Native Americans. But the trace from Limestone, now Maysville, to Lexington was only relatively easy. For a city to be founded and flourish in the late eighteenth and early nineteenth centuries so far from water transport demanded that the site have very special qualities. What makes this land so fine and desirable? Geologically, it is the karst topography appearing as a fertile limestone-based plateau. Thus we have the beautiful "rolling" landscape which, in aspect, reminds many of Kent in England. Native Americans had long cherished this place as one rich in provisions for life that best served man when left in its natural state. The last settlement of Native Americans in the region in historical times is reputedly the Shawnee community they called Eskippakithiki ("blue licks place") in what is today Clark County. Salt "licks" were a great attraction for wildlife. The Shawnee stopped living here in the mid-eighteenth century and from that time are considered to have shared the region with a number of other tribes as a hunting ground free of tribal conflict. This romantic notion does seem reasonable. The very word "Kentucky" means "meadow lands" in several Native American tongues and thus would likely have denoted this area in particular.

Early European visitors saw a savannah from which rose mighty Bur oaks and named it for the bluish cast to the flowering grass (*Poa pratensis*) that partially carpeted it. This is a rare sight now, except when the grass is allowed to go to seed. The pasturage created by this grass was noted early on to be beneficial to the livestock, especially horses, grazing upon it and ingesting the minerals peculiar to the soil. The many streams enhancing this fertility, some intermittently running underground, empty into the Kentucky River. From the air, the perimeter of the inner Bluegrass can be clearly discerned. It is this "inner" Bluegrass—a relatively small area around the city of Lexington, a site named in 1776, encompassing parts of Fayette County and those counties touching it—that we who live here deem the true Bluegrass Country.

While Kentucky and the Bluegrass are commonly characterized as "Southern" today, I feel that this is somewhat misleading. Our cultural foundation could more properly be deemed mid-Atlantic with strong ties to Philadelphia and Baltimore. Our farms were not the plantations of the Deep South, although they were often linked by ownership. Tragically, Kentucky was a literal breeding ground for slavery, even though its rural economy was not well suited to that horrific institution. Our very state song, the beautiful "My Old Kentucky Home" for which we always stand, is about human beings being sold "down river." But the lifestyle here was of a different nature. Transylvania University in Lexington, tracing its foundation to eighteenth-century Presbyterian institutions of learning, was, in its early years, responsible, I feel, for the cultural atmosphere enjoyed by this "Athens of the West."

Today, the Bluegrass is amazingly cosmopolitan. Some of the owners of properties depicted herein are quite satisfied with conserving what they have found themselves to possess while others have enhanced their environments in idiosyncratic ways. Estersohn often shows "the way we live now" (with a nod to Trollope) with what we have been given. A common link is the hospitality to be enjoyed at each. Seven sites depicted are open to the public and exhibit interpretations of, and even departure from, the typical "house museum" concept. Estersohn has photographed six working farms with a notable degree of diversity. Each presents a lifestyle peculiar to the landowner. These are sites where Thoroughbred and Standardbred horses, cattle, and other livestock, and crops and ornamental plantings are variously cultivated. Four residences are in what is now urban Lexington. Contemporary life and taste gives vitality to these old homes. All are loved by an eclectic mix of friends. Images of the Iroquois Hunt hint at the close relationship, sometimes quite physical, between people and the land.

Such a singular environment should be lived with and nurtured rather than conquered. Today Lexington and the Bluegrass are in the process of a revitalization and conservation of elements that were wounded but not killed by misguided attempts at progress or greed. Current dangers have prompted the World Monuments Fund to include the Bluegrass in the one hundred most endangered sites on earth. This is a rather dark recognition of how important the place really is. While many who have been here for a long time may bemoan what is gone, we are very pleased when newcomers and visitors express their delight in just how much of our heritage has been maintained in comparison with other places. You are invited to see for yourselves Pieter Estersohn's inspiration.

ASHLAND

LEXINGTON

1809-11, REBUILT AFTER 1856

HENRY CLAY IS KNOWN AS one of the greatest American statesmen, a United States senator and speaker of the House. He was dubbed the Great Compromiser for his pivotal role in keeping the Union together during the first half of the nineteenth century. But at Ashland, his 660-acre estate on the outskirts of Lexington, Clay was also a cutting-edge farmer and breeder of successful racehorses.

Lincoln called Clay "my beau ideal of a statesman." But Clay's own ideal was life on his farm, where he said he exchanged "the strife of politics" for a "passion for rural occupations." He once wrote that he was "better off than Moses" who "died in sight of, without reaching, the promised land." Clay began creating his own promised land not long after he moved from Virginia to the young state of Kentucky. After he married Lucretia Hart, daughter of one of Kentucky's most prominent pioneering families, he began acquiring land in 1804. By 1809, the center block of the house, named Ashland after the ash groves on the property, was complete. In 1811, Clay asked his good friend Benjamin Latrobe, architect of the U.S. Capitol as well as the nearby Pope Villa, to design two L-shaped wings.

The farm's cash crop was hemp, and there was a great variety of livestock including the Hereford cattle Clay was the first to import into America. He also bred and raced Thoroughbreds, adopting the Whig party's colors of buff and blue for his racing silks.

Ashland's Colonial Revival garden was created by the Garden Club of Lexington in 1950.

Preceding pages
A silver trophy is displayed in front of the Palladian window in the second-floor hall.

Ashland today is a five-part Federal-style structure with Italianate details.

The Eastlake staircase, installed by the McDowells, replaced an earlier elliptical design.

Overleaf
The drawing room features a portrait of George Washington and his family given to Henry and Lucretia Clay in her honor.

Ashland was completely rebuilt after Clay's death in 1852 by his son James. Built with a particularly porous brick, the structure was also likely damaged in the New Madrid earthquake and aftershocks of 1811–12. When James bought the house from his mother, he found it in such unstable shape that he was forced to raze the structure and rebuild, salvaging as many pieces of the house as possible. Architect Thomas Lewinski essentially recreated the house on the original foundation, incorporating some of the Italianate and Greek revival details popular at the time and using a sturdy dark red brick.

Ashland passed out of the Clay family when James fled to Montreal during the Civil War. In 1882 Henry Clay's granddaughter Anne Clay McDowell bought Ashland with her husband, Henry Clay McDowell (so named in honor of her grandfather). The McDowells added the Eastlake and Aesthetic design elements to the interiors, renovated the stables (where they concentrated on Standardbreds), and restored the grounds, especially Clay's Walk, a winding footpath around the back lawn, where the great man was said to have strolled when planning his speeches.

When the McDowells died, their oldest child, Nannette McDowell Bullock, moved in with her family and helped create the Henry Clay Memorial Foundation to preserve her great grandfather's legacy, including Ashland and the seventeen acres it now sits on. Since 1950, the house and grounds have been open to the public as a museum.

Preceding pages, left
This painting is a copy of a portrait of Henry Clay that illustrates his political plan, known as the American System.

Preceding pages, right
The dining room.

Opposite and right
James Clay is thought to have re-created the library as part of his rebuilding of the estate. The paneling is black and white walnut. The serpent gasolier was installed by the McDowells.

Overleaf, left
Henry Clay's hatbox, which contained his top hat when he traveled, is stamped with his name and address.

Overleaf, right
Henry Clay loved his bed and used it for about twenty years. The quilt is a reproduction of one given to Clay by the Whig Ladies of Philadelphia.

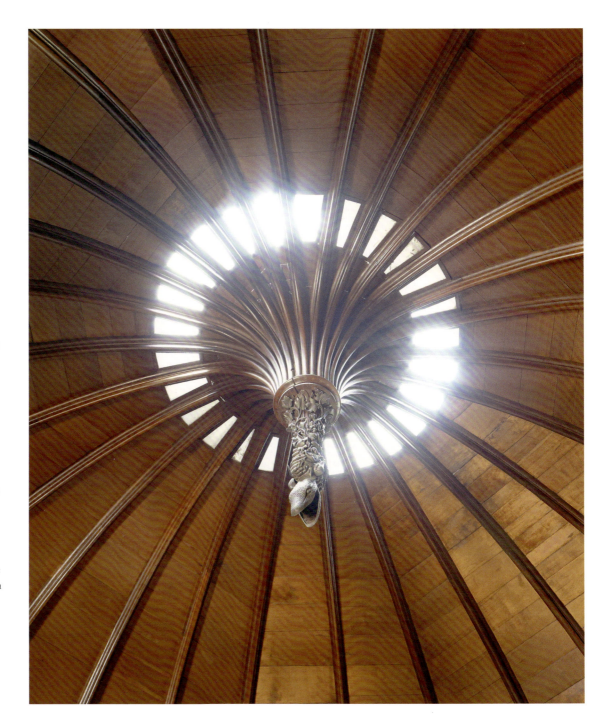

SIMPSON FARM

PARIS

1785

THE EARLY STONE house in the area still known as Kiser Station is one of the most important in Bourbon County. Built by John Kiser in 1785, when the county was still a part of Virginia, it also served as a makeshift courthouse the year after it was built.

In 1780 Kiser brought his family from Maryland by way of Virginia to settle on land where Cooper's Run pours into Stoner Creek. Despite the fact that he and other nearby settlers built a fort for protection against the Indian threat, four of his family members were killed in an attack in 1787. Undeterred, Kiser stayed on, acquiring one thousand acres on which he ran a grist mill, a saw mill, and a distillery.

Kiser's original two-story house feature wide plank floors and an unusual flat Georgian mantel. In the early nineteenth century, a one-and-a-half-story wing was added, and the house was re-oriented to face the creek. The wing consists of a large parlor with an elaborate mantel and a spacious stair hall. A stone smokehouse and a large log barn still exist on the property.

The house stayed in the Kiser family until 1952, after which it changed hands twice. Since 1965, the house has been owned by Pat and Laurance Simpson, who uncovered the wall painting above the parlor mantel. The painting, discovered when the Simpsons peeled back layers of wallpaper, depicts a large vase of roses with hummingbirds hovering among the branches. Though none of the furnishings are original to the house, the Simpsons have filled it with a fitting mix of English and American antiques inherited from their own families. Mr. Simpson's mother, Elizabeth Simpson, is the author of two important books on early Kentucky homes, *Bluegrass Houses and Their Traditions* and *The Enchanted Bluegrass*.

The house is built of local limestone most likely quarried on the farm. The two-story block is the original structure; the one-and-a-half-story addition was built between 1800 and 1810.

Preceding pages
A small shed built off of the log barn is used to store farm tools. Pat Simpson built the stone wall and laid the brick floor herself, while the wooden beams of the log barn are original.

Above
The cherry cabinets and Georgian mantel in the living room are late eighteenth century. Over the mantel is a mural, which was uncovered when layers of wallpaper were removed during the Simpsons' renovation.

Opposite
This mantel has special resonance for Pat Simpson. Her father attempted to purchase it from the Kisers in 1925. When they declined to sell, he had it copied for his own house in Lexington, where Pat grew up. When Pat moved into Kiser Station in the 1960s, she was surprised to find the original of the mantel of her childhood home.

Overleaf
The former dining room, now affectionately known as the "old folks' room," contains a more traditional mantel. Above it hangs a portrait of Jacob Spears, a relative who was killed in a barroom brawl. A portrait of Laurance Simpson rests on the desk.

Left
The original front hall is now used as the dining room. The Victorian staircase was added in the late nineteenth century.

Opposite
An Audubon print of the sandwich tern sits above a flat Georgian mantel in the kitchen.

Overleaf
The downstairs bedroom, known as the "boys' room," is in the "new" wing of the house.

Second overleaf, left
The upstairs bedroom is in the older part of the house. The fireplace and closets are original to the structure, and the locally crafted bed belonged to Pat Simpson's mother.

Second overleaf, right
Sunlight from the south spills into the stairwell. The enclosure at the top of the stair is repurposed wood from the original staircase.

WELCOME HALL

VERSAILLES

1792, EXPANDED C. 1820

HOME TO SEVEN GENERATIONS OF THE GRADDY FAMILY, Welcome Hall is one of the finest examples of an early Kentucky estate. Construction probably started in 1789, three years before statehood, by John Long Sr., and was completed by 1792. The house took shape as a Penn Plan of hand-cut limestone quarried on the farm, with 24-inch thick walls surrounding five rooms on two floors.

In 1806, after many years as a successful farmer and father, with his wife, Mary Haynes, of twelve children, Long decided to sell the house, now enlarged with a wing defined by dormer windows on the east side. His advertisement in the Frankfort, Kentucky, newspaper *Western World* described an "elegant stone dwelling house" with "horse mill, distillery, orchards and other appurtenances of a well-established pioneer plantation."

For reasons unknown, the transaction was delayed until 1816, when Jesse Graddy, great-great-great-grandfather-in-law of Kitty Graddy Tonkin, the present owner, bought the homestead for his eldest son, William Lee Graddy. During William Lee's tenure, the pedimented, columned portico at the main entrance was added along with the second-story veranda and a Greek Revival L-shaped wing. Each of the three sections of the house has a second floor, but they are not connected, being closed off by the original limestone walls. Upon William Lee's death, the house stayed in the family, few of whom made great changes. As Richard S. DeCamp, author of *The Bluegrass of Kentucky*, comments, "Thank goodness, generations of Graddys had so much land to take care of that they never got around to keeping it stylistically up-to-date. For well over two hundred years, Welcome Hall has gone unscathed and retains its original integrity and charm." A gazebo was built in the garden in the 1930s by landscape designer Henry Fletcher Kenney under the

A Shaker rocking chair welcomes visitors to the guest cottage, which was originally slave quarters. It faces the main house's extensive porches.

Preceding pages
The Greek Revival room at the front of the house is furnished with stenciled Sheraton chairs and a cherry drop-leaf table made in Kentucky. The expansion of Welcome Hall is evident on the entrance facade, where the original center block is flanked by two later wings.

watchful eye of Louise Garrett Graddy, mistress of the house four generations ago, and an upstairs bathroom was added in the same timeframe.

Louise Garrett Graddy worked to preserve the interior, which features fine hand-carved mantels and beautiful woodwork that, according to Lexington historian J. Winston Coleman, "attest to the skill of the early Kentucky craftsmen," regional furniture, and layouts that reveal the lives of the occupants.

Several outbuildings still stand—a two-room slave cabin, now converted into a guesthouse, a store house where firewood is kept, and a dairy used as an apple bin. Obsolete today but necessary for a self-sufficient country estate in its heyday, there are also a carriage house, a smokehouse, a springhouse, and an icehouse. Of note is the discovery of an earthen-walled room below the floorboards of the original slave quarters, a safe place for runaway slaves to hide on their journey to freedom.

Ardent supporters of historic preservation, the current Graddy family members were proud to have their homestead listed on the National Register of Historic Places in 1975. It was absorbed into the Clifton-McCracken Pikes Rural Historic District, also on the National Register, in 1999.

Graddy family silver and porcelain are displayed on the sideboard and serving tables in the dining room.

A portrait of Jesse Graddy hangs over the fireplace in the paneled great hall. Early-nineteenth-century American wing chairs, designed to protect from drafts, sit on a Persian rug from the 1880s.

Left
Spoons crafted by a local 1820s silversmith rest on heirloom linen napkins.

Opposite
The Greek Revival sitting room includes a Federal-style fireplace fender, a tole coal scuttle, and mahogany Sheraton-style chairs upholstered in leather. The portrait is of Viola Graddy.

Opposite
Furnished with white-painted wicker, the open-air porch has been a favorite summertime gathering place for many generations of Graddys and their friends.

Right
Maintained for its historic significance but not used today, the brick smokehouse, topped with a split-wood shake roof, was built at the same time as the center block of the house.

BOTHERUM

LEXINGTON

1851

BOTHERUM HAS BEEN DESCRIBED one of the most outstanding examples of romantic architecture in America, and certainly, the story of its beginnings is a romantic one. Botherum was commissioned by Major Madison Conyers Johnson as a shrine to his wife, Sally Ann Clay Johnson, who died in childbirth in 1828. Johnson, a banker and lawyer, was a friend of Henry Clay, a confidante of Abraham Lincoln, and the model for Colonel Romulus Fields, one of the two main characters in James Lane Allen's novel *Two Gentlemen from Kentucky*. Sally Ann, a cousin of Henry Clay, was the beautiful sister of Cassius Clay, the prominent anti-slavery crusader and Lincoln's minister to Russia. When the house was completed, Johnson lived there alone.

The work of Lexington architect and builder John McMurtry, the one-story stone house was originally partially covered in stucco. Its U-shaped design encompassed a rear court that was later filled in to create a dining room. Botherum is an unusual combination of a classical exterior and a Gothic revival interior, although occasionally elements cross over. Stained glass panels in the front door are more typical of Gothic revival, for example.

Visitors enter the house through a very short hallway and pass through double doors into a vaulted reception room under a skylight. The recessed door leading into the library is supported by Ionic columns, but the octagonal drawing room beyond is pure Gothic revival with bay windows and a coved ceiling

The entrance facade shows the builder's inventive combination of period style elements and a classical Federal scale unusual in a mid-nineteenth-century dwelling.

Preceding pages
Ionic columns mark the opening between the reception room and the library.

enhanced by a plaster medallion of vines and flowers.

McMurtry has been described as a builder first and not so concerned with historical precedent, enabling him to so freely mix the two distinct styles. In fact, he asserted that all architecture derived from just two elements, the arch and the post and lintel. In his seminal book, *The Antebellum Architecture of Kentucky*, Clay Lancaster suggests, "Perhaps it was this ultracism coupled with long experience in building that gave him the audacity to create the most charming Romantic residence in Lexington."

One of the most charming touches is the octagonal cupola with a wrought-iron railing that was included at the behest of Johnson, an amateur astronomer. But the lookout is not the only quirk of the place. Johnson was reported to have hidden many a slave escaping to freedom via the underground railway in a safe haven beneath the original basement kitchen. He also had an early version of automatic gates: they opened and shut when a mechanism was tripped by carriage wheels passing over it.

The original 36-acre property is today only three-quarters of an acre, but it still contains the now-massive gingko tree given to Johnson by Henry Clay—one of the Botherum's many features that appealed to its current owners, Dale Fisher and Jon Carloftis, a noted garden designer. The two see themselves as stewards of the house that Johnson and his builder so lovingly created. "We want to clean it up and bring it alive," Carloftis said after the pair bought it in 2012. "We are going to preserve, not renovate."

Opposite
Gothic Revival elements on the interior inlcude the stained glass panels in the front door and the arched entrance to the principal reception room.

Overleaf
The principal reception room (left) and the entrance hall. The hall must have served multiple functions, and the sky light is important in this windowless space. Colors reflect the taste of a former owner.

Second overleaf
An original chandelier is seen against the plasterwork of the coved ceiling of the reception room.

SHAKER VILLAGE

PLEASANT HILL

1805–1910

THE SHAKER VILLAGE OF PLEASANT HILL was an active Shaker religious community from 1805 to 1910. Located just twenty-five miles outside of Lexington, it was founded by three missionaries sent west by Lucy Wright, the head of the parent community in New Lebanon, New York.

The Shaker movement was born in America when a handful of Shakers—members of the United Society of Believers in Christ's Second Appearing—came from England to escape religious persecution. After the Revolution, they settled in New York and began organizing believers into communities that would follow such doctrines as separation from the world, confession of sin, celibacy, and communal property. The Shakers were also known for their belief in the equality of the sexes and for their enthusiastic style of worship, which included singing and dancing, shaking, and speaking in tongues.

In 1805 the Ohio Valley of Kentucky was already home to a great many believers firmly in the grip of the Second Great Awakening, as well as the site of days-long revival meetings. Newspaper accounts of the ecstatic goings on had reached Lucy Wright, and when her missionaries made the thousand-mile trek to the area, they made many converts. One of them, a Mercer Country resident named Elisha Thomas, donated his 140-acre farm that would become the core of the new settlement. By the end of the first year, Shaker Hill was home to forty-four members who signed a covenant agreeing to common ownership of the property. At its height in the 1820s, the community had almost five hundred residents and had acquired more than four thousand acres of land.

The Centre Family dwelling was first occupied in September 1834. Only the state capitol was larger at that time. Shaker women entered at the left door, Shaker men at the right.

An arrow-back Windsor settee is centered on the second floor landing, between two interior staircases, the left for women and the right for men. Above is a rail of Shaker pegs for hanging furniture, implements, and garments. There are 3,000 pegs in the Centre Family dwelling.

Woodwork in the kitchen is painted "workshop red." A meal or flour chest is at left, and a flat Shaker broom hangs from a peg. Side chairs were brought in from "the world" in the 1850s to replace benches for dining.

The Shakers at Pleasant Hill cultivated garden seeds (to package and sell), broom corn (with which to make their handsome brooms), and fruit, which they either dried or preserved. Their products were in such demand that they regularly traveled as far as New Orleans to sell them—one year they reported sales of more than ten tons of preserves. The community also bred livestock, including Berkshire hogs, cattle, and Saxony sheep for wool, and engaged in selective breeding long before their neighbors adopted the practice. Unlike the Amish, the Shakers had no fear of technological advancement. Pleasant Hill had one of Kentucky's first municipal water systems, and powered their sophisticated water pumps (as well as early versions of our washing machines) by horses.

The order's Millennial Laws, laid down in 1821, included architectural standards that prohibited "odd or fanciful styles" as well as "beadings, moulding and cornices." The Shakers pioneered the principles of form and function, seeking also to create structures that would inspire a sense of serenity and grace. Essential to every meeting house was large uninterrupted floor space that would accommodate religious dances, and wood peg rails for hanging garments, hats, and baskets were a feature of most rooms. The Shakers also made their own furniture, including the ladder-back chairs that became so popular they acquired a patent for them.

Opposite
Although largely self-sufficient, Pleasant Hill's Shaker community would have brought these stoneware vessels in from "the world."

Above
Shaker ladder-back chairs hang from Shaker pegs in the kitchen. A Shaker bowl turned from one piece of wood rests on the table. Paneled reveals at the windows reveal the two-foot thickness of the exteriors walls.

Opposite
Both the Shaker side chair and rocker show the bulb finials characteristic of furniture made at Pleasant Hill. The chest is a typical example of Shaker casework construction. Furniture from Pleasant Hill, often of richly colored cherry wood, was not painted.

Above
An interior fanlight in the kitchen doorway shares light even when the door is closed.

Overleaf
These built-in chests of drawers were used to store winter clothes in the summer and summer clothes in the winter. Above the skylight is the cupola that crowns the building.

At Pleasant Hill, brick and stone buildings were neatly arranged along stone sidewalks and marked by wide lawns. The property is also the site of twenty-five miles of rock fences, the most extensive remaining in Kentucky. During the Civil War, the community came under occasional physical attack for their pacifist views and their official support of the Union, and they fed so many thousands of hungry soldiers that their resources were all but depleted. By 1900, only thirty-four members remained, and Pleasant Hill was formally dissolved in 1910.

In the ensuing years, the old meeting hall was used for everything from an automotive garage to a Baptist church. After World War II, area residents, including Thomas Merton, the writer, social activist, and monk at the nearby Abbey of Gethsemane in Bardstown, began to take an interest in preserving the place. In 1963, the Friends of Pleasant Hill was formed, and today, thirty-four of the original buildings sit on almost three thousand acres of land. Shaker Hill is the largest restored Shaker community in the country.

WARD HALL

GEORGETOWN

1853

WARD HALL, THE SUMMER HOME OF Mississippi planter Junius Ward, was once described by his nephew Henry Viley Johnson as "the finest place in Kentucky . . . a veritable palace surrounded by a fairy garden." The gardens may be long gone, but the house, the largest Greek revival structure in Kentucky, has lost none of its palatial appeal. Completed in 1857, Ward Hall occupies 12,000 square feet on four stories and is fronted by fluted Corinthian columns standing twenty-seven feet high. Widely considered one of the finest mid-nineteenth-century classical structures in America, Ward Hall is almost entirely intact.

The families of Junius Ward, and his wife, Matilda Viley, were among Kentucky's earliest pioneers and horse enthusiasts. At one time Ward, along with his brother-in-law, Captain Willa Viley, and two others, owned Lexington, one of the greatest racehorses of the second half of the nineteenth century and the era's most successful sire. Ward made his fortune farming cotton in the Mississippi Delta, the extraordinarily rich alluvial flood plain formed by the Yazoo and Mississippi Rivers. That area was still largely untamed when Ward bought his land ceded from the Choctaws. Ward Hall was built as a May-though-October residence where Ward, his wife, and their five surviving children could find respite from the heat and pestilence of the Mississippi Delta.

The house was almost entirely based on the designs of Minard Lafever, an architect whose 1829 and 1835 pattern books were largely responsible for the Greek Revival fever that spread throughout the country. It was designed by Major Thomas Lewinski, a British-born architect who arrived in central Kentucky in the 1830s, and erected by builder Taylor Buffington, to whom Ward is said to have paid $50,000 in gold with another $500 lingenap for a job well done. Originally situated on more than five hundred acres, the house boasted an innovative plumbing system

Opposite
The view from the second-floor hall window extends past the highly articlulated cast-iron capitals and hand-fluted columns supporting the portico to the front lawn.

Preceding pages
The tripartite arrangement of openings surrounding the front door is based on a plate from one of Minard Lefever's pattern books.

Overleaf
Approached by heroic steps, the majestic mansion sits on a brushed and hammered coquina limestone base.

The nautilus-chambered, double-ellipical staircase rises from the west center bay of the entry hall to the third floor. Detailing includes a denticulated cornice, an egg-and-dart molding, and bead-and-reel accents.

that collected rainwater from the roof and a greenhouse of rare tropical plants with a carbide lighting system. But it is the stunning proportions and lavish attention to detail on such a grand scale that makes Ward Hall so important.

A generous center hall, fourteen feet wide and sixty-five feet long, runs through the first and second floors. To the left of the first-floor hall are two reception rooms and a dining room while two rooms on the right, the library and sitting room, were reserved for the family. Five bedrooms, one of which could serve as a "travelers room," make up the second floor. The third floor has one formal room and two attic spaces that originally were intended to be finished. The basement includes the office/butler's room, servants' dining room, servants' sleeping rooms, warming kitchen, laundry room, pantries, and wine cellar.

The exceptional state of preservation of the interiors extends to the hardware—Sheffield silver in the public rooms and cast iron in the service spaces. The plasterwork in the two reception rooms and hallway retain the original tinted colors, a process known as distemper. Shelving in the dining room cupboard, basement pantries, and bedroom presses is also intact.

The Ward Hall Preservation Foundation, led by Board Chairman David Stuart, has taken care to furnish the house with period items, but none of the furniture is original to the house. Junius Ward's reversals of fortune after the Civil War forced a court-ordered sale at public auction of the house itself, and the contents were subsequently dispersed. The war was also unkind to Kentucky's racehorses—most were conscripted from the state's many horse farms to serve as mounts—but Ward's horse, Lexington, fifteen years old and blind at the outbreak of battle, was hidden away. His skeleton is now displayed at the Museum of the Horse just eight miles from Ward Hall.

In the dining room, folding shutters recede into the casements when not in use. The silver closet features a massive Lefever enframement with gilded egg-and-dart and filigree ornament in the pediment.

Opposite
Flanking the carved carrara marble mantel in the front reception room are portraits of Junius Ward and Matilda Viley Ward.

Right
The private family sitting room on the first floor incorporates overscaled woodwork after Lefever's designs.

Bedrooms were set up to accommodate families and their children in the same space.

Above
A massive tester bed dominates this generous bedroom with ample space for sitting.

Opposite
The buttery, one of several pantries in the basement, is a rare survivor.

MAPLE HILL
C. V. WHITNEY FARM

LEXINGTON

1796, EXPANDED 1840S

SYNONYMOUS WITH THE BEST THOROUGHBRED RACING in Bluegrass Country and generations of great wealth, power, and philanthropy, the C. V. Whitney Farm is crowned by Maple Hill, a special place with a unique history.

While the farm was established in 1915 by Harry Payne Whitney, when he transported his horses there from his New Jersey stable, the story of Maple Hill began two centuries earlier. In 1784, Elizabeth and Joseph Hale Rogers traded their Culpeper County, Virginia, plantation for a parcel of Kentucky farm land and set out with their eight children and household goods, including their blacksmith and family cook, crates of whiskey, beautiful chandeliers, rugs and drapes, forty-two slaves, and all manner of livestock in a cortege of twelve covered wagons. Over steep mountains, down the Ohio River on flatboats, and then bouncing over buffalo trails, they finally arrived at what would be their new home, a spacious, log-and-frame house. The brick residence, which makes up the heart of Maple Hill, was built nearby by their son John in 1796 for his family, and over time it grew to include a second floor with a master bedroom, a parlor for his wife, Sarah, and an office for him. All its rooms are used today, albeit some for different purposes than originally intended.

Willis and Harriette Muir took up residence in 1841. It was he who introduced horses to the farm, breeding and racing trotting horses and selling saddle and livery stock. Harriette was a vivacious hostess, and she expanded the house for her elegant soirées with a grand stairway in the entrance, a third parlor with expansive bay window and handcarved woodwork, a formal dining room, two bedrooms upstairs and a sitting room highlighted by a gilded, antique French desk still used today.

The stately facade of the Federal-style house is white-painted brick sparked with simple, wood-shuttered windows and always, an American flag.

Preceding pages
The front door opens into a welcoming hall, with elegant French furniture and a needlepoint rug. A Swedish mora clock stands in the corner.

Overleaf
The formal living room with its curved bay window presents a lively mix of furniture inherited from Gertrude Vanderbilt and European and Asian pieces acquired on Mrs. Whitney's extensive travels or at auction.

Above
An informal bar is lined with photographs of many of the Whitneys' Thoroughbreds and their racing triumphs.

Opposite
A photograph in the trophy room shows Sonny and Marylou Whitney with the Nixons and the Reagans at the Kentucky Derby. Flanking it is are trophies topped by jockeys wearing the Whitney racing colors.

The Civil War swept through the region leaving destruction in its midst. But in 1872, when life had settled down, Mary Kenney, a Muir by marriage, moved in. Out went the elder Muirs' Georgian look, and in came Victoriana, as well as such useful items as a rainwater-collection system complete with pump.

In 1931 Joe and Bliss McDowell became the owners, toning down the decor with a simpler look and adding such conveniences as a furnace, central heating system and three bathrooms. Revamping the arbor, rose bed and herb and vegetable gardens, as well as the interiors, Mrs. McDowell returned Maple Hill to the icon of style it had once been. Finally, C. V.

The pool is placed within a classical setting with a glazed roof and generous arched openings that open the space to the landscape.

Whitney bought Maple Hill in 1951, but rather than moving in, rented it out for seven years.

By the time Marylou Whitney arrived as a bride in 1958, the house was, as she recalls, "a dilapidated red brick farmhouse flanked by a tangle of chicken coops and pigsties with rotting posts, rickety steps, and worm-eaten floorboards."

Challenged by her husband to fix it up, she jumped into the project with passion. It took three years and two months, but she brought her vision to life: a rambling Kentucky farmhouse with "all its crazy twists and turns intact." While preserving some of the odder characteristics, such as three windowless rooms, Mrs. Whitney made extensive changes inside and out: a children's wing with four bedrooms and two baths was put on the second floor, a glass-topped Romanesque atrium housing an Olympic-size swimming pool was added, and a Federal-style facade was constructed. The smoke house was turned into a painting studio, the slave house became a two-floor guest cottage, an oak-paneled library from a French château was installed, and a log cabin that had belonged to Daniel Boone's wife, Rebecca, was bought and rebuilt as a chapel on the property. Among the highlights was the unearthing of a section of the Underground Railroad connecting Maple Hill with the slave cabin.

Furnished as only she could—"Provenance is not important. If I like something I buy it, and store it 'til I find the perfect location"—there is everything from fine French furniture found in antique shops and auction houses on her worldwide travels, marble sculpture by her mother-in-law, Gertrude Vanderbilt Whitney, and a notable collection of equestrian paintings.

"Maple Hill has known sadness," says Whitney, " but it is a very happy house. A much-loved house." An avid horsewoman, she continues to breed and race winning Thoroughbreds and has been awarded numerous industry honors for her work on behalf of the sport.

Opposite
A portrait of Mrs. Whitney by Delos Palmer hangs above the marble fireplace at on end of the living room.

Right
A photograph of the Whitneys with New York socialite Anne Slater at one of Venice's famed masked balls.

Overleaf
The dining room is decorated in soothing blue tones.

WAVELAND

LEXINGTON

1847

WAVELAND WAS ONCE situated on two thousand acres of land said to have been surveyed by Daniel Boone for his nephew and namesake, Daniel Bryan, a frontiersman and Revolutionary War soldier who was also a poet and historian. In the 1780s, Bryan built a simple stone house on the property, where he operated a number of enterprises, including a gun shop, a grist mill, a blacksmith shop, a paper mill, and a distillery. He also built a Baptist church and established a school for girls.

When Bryan's son Joseph inherited the property, he tore down the original house and, inspired by the work of Lexington architect and builder John McMurtry, set out to build a far grander Greek Revival mansion. Lumber for the project was milled from trees on the grounds, the bricks came from clay dug and fired on site, and Waveland's blacksmith shop wrought the iron. Even the stone for the foundation was quarried at nearby Tyrone on the Kentucky River.

The house is still considered one of the finest examples of Greek Revival architecture in Kentucky. A monumental Ionic portico graces the front facade, and the front door is topped by a frieze that replicates the north entrance to the Erechtheum on the Acropolis. Two-story porches run almost the entire length of each side of the house, while the interior features a wide center hall and fourteen-foot ceilings. The name Waveland was inspired by the surrounding fields of grain and hemp that rippled in "waves" when the wind blew through.

When Joseph Bryan's son, Joseph Henry Bryan, became

The pairs of ionic columns flanking the entrance are brick overlaid with stucco and topped by whitewashed carved wood capitals.

Preceding pages
The door of Joseph Bryan's plantation office opens onto the lawn of Waveland. A painting of Goldsmith Abdullah, the famous racehorse, hangs over an Empire-style gaming table.

the owner of Waveland in 1887, he turned the property into one of the premier Thoroughbred and trotter farms in the state. Among Waveland's great horses were the celebrated sire Waveland Chief and Wild Rake. Bryan also built two racecourses on the property, but by 1884 his gambling debts had gotten the better of him, and he was forced to sell Waveland at auction.

In 1956 the University of Kentucky bought the house and two hundred acres to use as experimental farmland. The following year the house was turned into a museum and decorated in period style. Four outbuildings—the ice house, a slave quarter, a barn, and a smokehouse—also survive. Waveland's curator, Ron Bryant, is a descendant of the original family.

Above
Period-style wallpaper and draperies adorn the formal dining room. A portrait of Joseph Bryan presides over the space.

Opposite
In the adjacent sitting room is a ladder back chair, called the Boone chair. Daniel Boone brought the chair, crafted by his father, Squire Boone, from Pennsylvania to Kentucky in 1779.

Preceding pages
The decor of the formal parlor reflects the style of the 1850s. The sofa belonged to the Bryans, and a portrait of Elizabeth Turner Bryan, the wife of the pioneer Daniel Bryan, hangs above the piano.

Left
A mid-nineteenth-century French Gothic bookcase houses the Bryans' collection of history, theology, and agriculture books.

Opposite
Joseph and Margaret Bryan's bed is in the Empire style. The curtain hangings of the canopy are all handmade.

The kitchen was located in the slave quarters, which was a separate two-story brick structure set off from the main house. The floorboards, enormous planks of burr oak, are original to the house. Strips of wood were mounted on the walls in order to hang kitchen tools.

Right
A corncob pipe rests on a mantel in the common room of the slave quarters.

Opposite
A dining table in the slave quarters is set with an old Tudor mug, which was handed down from the family to the slaves, and a hand-carved wooden pitcher.

Right and opposite
A Friendship quilt, made by the Bryans' slaves, is embroidered with the initials of the slaves who lived at Waveland and their friends. The quilt covers a straw-filled mattress on which children slept.

Overleaf
The vegetable garden, surrounded by a split rail fence, has grown heirloom produce since the 1840s.

ELLEY VILLA

LEXINGTON

1850–51

LIKE WARD HALL AND JANUARY HOUSE, Elley Villa was built as the summer home of a Deep South landowner, in this case Mississippi cotton planter William Elley, whose wife Louisa had grown up in the nearby Pope Villa.

Built in 1851, it was based on a design in *The Architecture of Country Houses* by Andrew Jackson Downing, which had been published the year before. Downing, an advocate of Gothic Revival style in the United States, wrote charming essays that accompanied his plans, lovingly laying out the way of life to be enjoyed in each. About the pattern most closely approximating Elley Villa, he wrote: "A sensible, solid, unpretending country house, with an air of substantial comfort and refinement, not overpowered by architectural style, but indicating intelligent, domestic life in the country." Elley Villa turned out to be the southernmost structure built of one of Downing's designs.

Downing stressed that while his designs were Gothic or pointed, they weren't copies of foreign houses. Instead they were very much geared toward practical life in the Middle United States. He references Elley Villa's "broad and massive veranda," its "steep roof, to . . . afford a well-ventilated attic," its "tasteful or convenient appendages of conservatory for plants on one side and kitchen offices on the other." The elaborately carved tracery windows that marked European Gothic houses were exchanged for plain windows with wide-slatted shutters, which would regulate light and air "in summer more perfectly than any other contrivance."

Elley Villa was home to a Mississippi planter, a Civil War judge, and a Civil War general. In later years it was called Aylesford, after owner Col. Oliver P. Alford, who operated a large horse farm on its surrounding acreage. The current owners, Martha and James Birchfield, restored both the house and the original name.

Though paddocks, a racetrack, and various dependencies existed behind the house in the nineteenth century, Elley Villa eventually fell on hard times. When Martha and James Birchfield bought the house in 1985, it had been condemned. Today, the exterior is painted the soft fawn shade that Downing encouraged, and the long entrance hall, encompassing the library (when the great paneled doors are opened) and marked by a large bay window, retains the "elegance" the designer envisioned. But the Birchfields haven't completely toed the line. "The house should be filled with rococo furniture," Martha Birchfield says, "but Empire is easier to find in Kentucky." Instead they came up with a ingenious narrative to justify their handsome collection of neoclassical pieces: "The young Mrs. Elley moved in with her mama's cast-offs from Pope Villa, her childhood home."

Above
Front hall.

Opposite
The original library, now used as a dining room, is decorated with prints of Strawberry Hill, the Gothic Revival country house of Horace Walpole.

Overleaf
Works of art in the front parlor include a gold-ground painting by Victor Hammer and a color lithograph of the horse Kentucky by Edward Troye. Kentucky belonged to Leonard Jerome, grandfather of Winston Churchill.

On the marble mantel in the front parlor are an ormolu and crystal garniture and two photographs of a Victorian gentleman.

The cherry wood two-piece banquet table with rope-twist legs is thought to be a Kentucky piece. The two portrait engravings depict Kentucky's renowned political favorite, Henry Clay. Over the mantel are engravings in keeping with the Gothic Revival details of the carved marble and the cast iron fireback.

Opposite
Flanking the dining room china closet are portraits of Mrs. Elley's uncle Vice-President Richard M. Johnson, hung above a White House dinner invitation (left), and her sister-in-law, poetess Rosa Vertner Johnson, above a note from Henry Clay.

Above
In the rear parlor is a self-portrait of Lexington artist T. S. Noble, first director of the Cincinnati Art Academy. Two Gothic Revival side chairs attributed to J. & J. W. Meeks face the table; behind is a bust of Lafayette, famed visitor to Lexington in 1825.

WARWICK

HARRODSBURG

1809–11

WARWICK, ALSO KNOWN AS the Moses Jones House, is located just twelve miles north of Harrodsburg, the oldest settlement in Kentucky. The house, built by Jones between 1809 and 1811, is notable for its elegant front portico, which was very likely the first in the state on a residential building.

Jones's saga illustrates the wild and woolly nature of frontier Kentucky. In the 1780s, his family emigrated west from Virginia with about two hundred others on a flotilla of flatboats. At the age of seven, while on an expedition with his uncles to scout for home sites, Jones was captured by the Chickasaws with whom he lived for nine years. When he learned that his father was living at Warwick Landing on the Kentucky River, he joined him; after his father died, Jones bought land at Warwick with his inheritance.

After his marriage to Mary Henderson in 1804, Jones built a one-and-a-half story Federal house with bricks he made and laid himself. The hall-and-parlor plan was similar to seventeenth-century houses in Virginia and New England, with the hall serving as the living room and the parlor serving as the master bedroom, while children slept in the two chambers upstairs. Jones, a cabinetmaker who made some of the house's furniture, also carved the classical hall and parlor mantels, both of which feature basketwork relief on the edge of the shelf.

Architectural historian Clay Lancaster added a clapboard addition distinct from the brick of the original Federal-era house. The pediment of his portico replicates that of the older structure, and the columns have a similar though more slender vase-like profile. The Tea Pavilion, at right, is a folly with a domed octagonal tearoom, a dining room with bookshelves, and a small kitchen.

Preceding pages
An attic bedroom in the original house.

Above
A view from the hall to the parlor. Frames extend above the doors to bring them to window height. Stairs behind the gray door at left rise to an attic bedroom.

Opposite
A corbeled vault marks twin stairways to two separate attic bedrooms for sons and daughters. Moses Jones, a cabinetmaker among many skills, may have carved the hall mantel beyond. The ash wood floors are original.

Opposite
The author of *Architectural Follies in America*, Clay Lancaster was charmed by the idea of creating them. His three-story octagonal Warwick Tower contains an elliptical parlor-dining room, a kitchen, three bedrooms, two baths, and a storage area for his research files.

Overleaf
Lancaster's Warwick Publications are displayed in the Tea Pavilion. A scholar of both American and Asian art and culture, Lancaster combined historic American architecture with oriental decorative elements.

The house was preserved by various Jones relatives until the 1970s when new owners bought it as a weekend house and added plumbing and electricity. In 1978 Warwick was purchased by the preservationist, teacher, author, and architectural historian Clay Lancaster, who had included the house in his book *Antebellum Architecture of Kentucky*. A native of Lexington and an expert on the nineteenth-century Kentucky architect and builder John McMurtry, Lancaster was on the faculty of Columbia University and served as the curator of Prospect Park in Brooklyn, the second great New York park designed by Frederic Law Olmsted. His fields of interest and expertise were extraordinarily wide ranging. His publications include *The Japanese Influence in America* and *The American Bungalow* as well as several books on Nantucket and charming children's books.

After he bought Warwick, Lancaster added a small wing with a library and master bath, and in the tradition of Moses Jones, he carved the new mantels himself. On the grounds, he added acreage for a nature preserve as well as charming follies of his own design. A Georgian tea pavilion houses Warwick Publications, which still publishes his books, and an arts and crafts style picture gallery was built to display his drawings and paintings. Warwick Tower is a two-story guesthouse modeled on the Tower of the Winds, an octagonal tower, probably first century, on the agora in Athens.

Before he died in 2000, Lancaster set up the Warwick Foundation, which maintains the house and grounds.

LIBERTY HALL

FRANKFORT

1796

AFTER JOHN BROWN became Kentucky's first senator, he bought four acres of land in Frankfort on which he built Liberty Hall. Brown likely designed the house himself, and the building shows a sophisticated understanding of the Federal style. The exterior is made of bricks locally fired from clay dug out of what is now the cellar. Brown, the Virginia-born son of Irish immigrants, is often referred to as the Father of Kentucky. When the Revolutionary War interrupted his studies at the College of New Jersey (now Princeton), he finished his degree at the College of William and Mary. After a stint in Thomas Jefferson's law office, he began his own practice in Danville—in what was then the county of Kentucky—and it was there that he began his political career, serving first as a representative of the County of Kentucky in the Virginia Legislature from 1784 to 1788. During that time, 1787-88, he served as a delegate from Virginia to the Continental Congress. When the Constitution became effective, Brown was twice elected to the House of Representatives as a congressman from Virginia and introduced the petition for Kentucky statehood. When Kentucky became a state in 1792, Brown resigned and was appointed senator of his new state.

Brown was in the Senate when he married Margaretta Mason of New York City and began the house in Frankfort. The family, which by then included infant son Mason, moved into Liberty Hall in 1801, even though construction was not fully completed. Glass would not be installed in the windows until 1803. Even so, the house was grand, featuring an enormous ballroom on the second floor that was divided to create separate rooms in 1818. Brown also built a number of outbuildings on the property, including a kitchen and smokehouse, and Margaretta installed an extensive garden between the house and the Kentucky River. The early garden featured fruit trees and vegetables, of course, but also climbing roses the young Mrs. Brown brought with her from New York.

The back porch of Liberty Hall leads to the formal gardens. Margaretta Brown referred to this porch as "the piazza."

Preceding pages
The impressive central hallway has thriteen-foot ceilings and grained woodwork to resemble mahogany.

In 1805, Brown lost his senate seat and retired permanently to Liberty Hall. Two years before his death in 1837, he divided his estate between his two surviving sons, giving Liberty Hall to Mason and building the new house for Orlando. For the second house, which is designed in the Greek Revival style, Brown commissioned Gideon Shryock, architect of the Kentucky State Capitol. Brown descendants lived in Liberty Hall until 1934 and in the Orlando Brown House until 1955. Today both houses are owned and operated as museums by the National Society of Colonial Dames of America in the Commonwealth of Kentucky.

Opposite
Lush gardens include flower, herb, and vegetable beds. Many varieties of trees, such as Cooper Beech, Gingko, Holly and Northern Catalpa dot the four-acre grounds.

Above
Liberty Hall is one of the finest examples of early Federal-era architecture in Kentucky with its symmetrical form and fine Palladian window.

The dining room is interpreted to 1825-35. The Old Paris style dinner service was purchased by Mason Brown (1799-1867), the son of Senator John Brown, in New Orleans in 1844. The set contains more than 300 pieces.

Opposite
The intricate carved detail on the top portion of the door frame in the parlor indicates that this was the most formal room in the house.

Above
The set of Fancy chairs, c. 1815, in the parlor belonged to Margaretta and John Brown.

Opposite
The original ballroom on the second floor was used as temporary storage during the recent renovation.

Above
In the first floor bedroom is a cherry wing chair dating to 1810, a rare example of an early upholstered Kentucky chair.

The detached kitchen was conntected to the main house by a breezeway. The blue-and- white canton china dates to 1810-20.

Overleft, right
The breezeway between the kitchen and the house. Firewood used in cooking demonstrations is stored there.

Overleaf, left
A second-floor space became a storage area during the renovation, which involved extensive research to determine appropriate paint finishes, wallpapers, draperies, and floor coverings for each room. The parlor, bedroom, and family parlor are now interpreted to 1805-15 and the dining room to 1825-35.

POPE VILLA

LEXINGTON

1810–11

WHEN JOHN POPE, a lawyer and United States senator from Kentucky, decided to build a villa in Lexington, he commissioned no less than Benjamin Latrobe, the man now called "America's first Architect," for the job. The British-born Latrobe had already designed the Bank of Pennsylvania in Philadelphia; when Pope met him in Washington he was in charge of completing the U. S. Capitol in his capacity as surveyor of public buildings, a position to which he had been appointed by President Thomas Jefferson.

The choice of Latrobe for what was essentially a summer home was a bold one—and may well have been a bribe of sorts to Pope's wife, Eliza. Her sister was married to John Quincy Adams, and the two women had grown up in the slightly more civilized environs of Regency London. Lexington may have had an opera house in 1810, but the town was also wild with rumors of a slave revolt.

Eliza Pope actively participated in the design of the house, and both architect and client were mindful of the senator's need to entertain and build his political base. The result, a perfectly proportioned brick cube with a domed rotunda in the center of the second story, remains unique in American architecture. The design was almost shockingly avant-garde for its time. The departures from the local vernacular begin at the front door, with its unique portico. But it was the interior that was truly revolutionary.

One of three surviving sheets of Benjamin Latrobe's original drawings for Pope Villa, now in the Library of Congress.

In the rotunda on the second floor a doorway to the dining room is at left and to the drawing room at right. A glass oculus above once illuminated this space with sunlight.

Latrobe despised the central hall plans of the day, and he referred to the halls themselves—which forced guests, members of the household, and servants to mix—as "common sewers." At Pope Villa, the servants' quarters, laundry, even the kitchen and bake house, were incorporated into the rear of the main house and hidden behind the first floor rooms. Thus, the public space contains a relatively short, square entrance hall with two receiving rooms, Senator Pope's office and Mrs. Pope's parlor, on either side. A graceful curved staircase, on the left, takes visitors to the rotunda and second-floor reception rooms and bedchambers, while the hidden staircase to the right allows the staff to move about invisibly.

The essence of the house, according to Latrobe scholar Patrick Snadon, is captured in Latrobe's scenic interior landscapes. His goal was to take people through the space as though they were touring a series of eighteenth-century English garden "rooms" and terraces—he referred to the light and shadow splashed across the walls as "scenery." The rotunda, with a sky-lit oculus and two statuary niches, offered a different kind of scenery. The curved walls of the apsidal-ended dining and drawing rooms joined in the center of the second floor.

Latrobe's plans for Pope Villa show that they were closely followed by local builders, but the Popes never saw them completely executed. When Senator Pope lost his re-election bid in 1813, he rented the house out to tenants, including one who referred in his diary to rooms that remained unplastered. When the Popes finally sold the place in 1829, it became the victim of at least four major renovations.

A fire in 1987 literally burned away some of the more egregious additions, and the almost austere elegance of Latrobe's original plan was again revealed. The Blue Grass Trust for Historic Preservation has undertaken the restoration Pope Villa, based on surviving details. Fragments of the original wooden mantels were found (they were replaced by marble mantels early on), original windows have been copied exactly, and a portico based on Latrobe's design has been added. Bits of a crown molding show small plaster balls clearly hand-rolled by local artisans, and layers of exterior paint were removed to reveal a soft terracotta brick red that is likely the original color. In the dining room, enough of the original wallpaper was uncovered to show that it was a blue-and-gray pattern now called Pebbles and Flowerpots.

Above
An exterior restoration by the Blue Grass Trust has revealed the Latrobe facade, long concealed by an eclectic accretion of gables, brackets, porches, iron railings, iron window hood moldings, and a cupola.

Opposite
Pope Villa's Federal-era entry was replaced in the mid-nineteenth century with this Greek Revival doorway.

A charred passage reveals damage from the 1987 fire. Of Pope Villa Judge Charles Kerr wrote in 1917, "That this stately old mansion, unless soon restored, must become the abode of bats and owls with all its ghostly accomplishments seems little less than a tragedy."

A view from the dining room into the drawing room. Both had rounded walls toward the center of the building. Here, on July 4, 1819, Maj. William S. Dallam entertained President James Monroe, Gen. Andrew Jackson, Gen. Isaac Shelby, and Col. Richard M. Johnson.

WALNUT HALL

LEXINGTON

1842

THE REVOLUTIONARY WAR BROUGHT DEVASTATION and despair to thousands of people, but it also gave a leg up to others. One of them was Colonel William Christian, who in 1777, was rewarded for his services with a 9,000-acre grant by brother-in-law, statesman Patrick Henry, a portion of it today graced by Walnut Hall.

After Christian was killed in a battle with marauding Indians, the vast property passed to his six children. Four hundred acres were sold to their brother-in-law Dr. Walter Warfield in 1806, and he later turned it over to Matthew Flournoy. The present Greek Revival style mansion—the first burned to the ground in the 1840s—was constructed by Flournoy's son Victor in 1842, from black walnut harvested on the estate. After Victor died with no heirs, two different owners—the bon vivant and horse breeder Major John Clark and Austrian engineer Rudolph Wieser— took up residence until 1892 when the house became the property of Lamon Vanderburgh Harkness, the great-grandfather of its current mistress, Margaret Jewett.

In the area to buy carriage horses, Harkness was so enamored with what he saw that he purchased the site and established Walnut Hall Stock Farm to breed standardbred horses, which he did with enormous success. Over the years, he grew the business to 5,000 acres, adding cattle, sheep, hogs and numerous crops. Upon his death in 1915, the establishment passed on to his daughter Lela, and her husband, Dr. Ogden M. Edwards, and the property has remained in the family ever since, with each generation bringing increased fame to his standardbred nursery.

The Greek Revival house is surrounded by old-growth bur oak, maple, and magnolia trees. The widow's walk offers a panoramic view of the property.

Preceding pages
In the stair hall are a carved wood bear from Bavaria and a moose head, a trophy of Lamon Vanderbrugh Harkness. The ornate, embossed wallpaper dates from the late 1800s.

Opposite
The mahogany ceiling in the entrance hall installed by L. V. Harkness, who also acquired the furniture on his travels around the world.

Above
At the end of the entrance hall is a curio cabinet filled with taxidermied birds given to Dr. Edwards, owner of the house in the early 1900s, as payment for his services as a pediatrician.

Overleaf, left
A portrait of L. V. Harkness hangs over the Gothic Revival mantel in the library.

"We grew up in Cincinnati," says Jewett of herself and her three sisters, two of whom own and run different sections of the land for standardbred breeding—"but we went to Walnut Hall on weekends and for summer vacations." Not much has changed in the intervening years, even since she took over Walnut Hall upon her mother's death in 1986. Still Victorian in spirit, it is distinguished by coffered ceilings, fireplaces in every room, and original wallcoverings.

The house, once painted white, is two stories high, with a hip roof and portico recessed behind slender Doric columns, one wing for the servants, another for the family, and a widow's walk. The modern conveniences Harkness installed in the 1890s include bathrooms that retain the look of the times, but no air conditioning or closets, not yet fashionable in his era.

Today, in addition to her horse-breeding activities, Margaret Jewett is involved in many philanthropic activities centering on equine welfare.

Overleaf, right
Enveloped in silk wall covering, the music room features a marble statue of the Crouching Venus and a collection of family photographs on a late nineteenth-century French table.

Second overleaf
The "nursery," used by all the family children including Mrs. Jewett, features silk wall covering, possibly from France, and twin brass beds that date back three generations.

OVERBROOK FARM

LEXINGTON

c. 1850

OVERBROOK FARM, ESTABLISHED BY BUSINESSMAN William T. Young in 1972, is one of the most famous Thoroughbred breeding farms in American history, with multiple wins in the Breeders' Cup, Preakness, Belmont Stakes, and Kentucky Derby. Inherited by his daughter, Lucy Young Hamilton and son, William T. Young Jr., upon his death in 2004, it has been Mrs. Hamilton's home base for more than a decade.

Little is known about the origins of the slate-roofed, white brick, Dutch Colonial except that it was built as a classic farmhouse in the mid-nineteenth century. While considerably more elegant and larger today, it is at heart simply a warm, inviting home.

Starting in the 1970s with architect Rebecca Van Meter, Mrs. Hamilton and her father oversaw a series of renovations, including the addition of bay windows in the breakfast room and library to bring in more sunlight and two substantial wings on either side of the house that provide both additional living space and the balance and presence lacking in the original building.

Today the house boasts a spectacular front-to-back hallway that gives out to the pool nestled between hornbeams. Formal rooms and two guest bedroom suites make up the first floor, with two bedroom suites above. Mrs. Hamilton's husband, the celebrated *New Yorker* cartoonist William Hamilton, works in a studio above the garage. Outbuildings include a chicken coop "to insure delicious soufflés," a brick cottage dating from the early eighteenth century, and a Moorish-detailed gazebo. One of the most picturesque structures that Mr. Young added

The original Dutch Colonial design is now enhanced with classical details, including the Palladian window on the second floor and a fanlight and side lights at the front door.

Above
In the entry hall, a bronze of the legendary sire Storm Cat, sculpted by Gwen Reardon, is placed below a massive Irish carved mahogany sideboard.

Opposite
The gazebo recalls Moorish designs in its graceful arches and tinkling bells suspended from the cupola.

is a covered bridge, reminiscent of those in New England. Traversing a stream, it was crafted so that Overbrook Farm's Storm Cat, one of the world's highest-priced sires, could easily access his paddock.

Lucy Hamilton has a great "eye," says Matthew Carter, her decorator, and she is drawn to Continental pieces, especially French and Italian. And while they often work closely together, she has no qualms about bringing in furnishings on her own as diverse as the neo-classical Georges Jacob chairs purchased from a Paris antiquaire and the tortoise-shell coffee table from the estate of legendary designer Mongiardino, both now in the living room. A mix of soft and bright shades, sophisticated yet comfortable furniture and an eclectic collection of paintings that includes works by Cézanne, Giorgio de Chirico, local naïf painter Henry Faulkner, and traditional English sporting paintings from the 1800s, enliven the rooms.

An exuberantly natural yet formal landscape surrounds the house. Densely planted, it creates privacy and frames superb views of grazing Thoroughbreds and rolling bluegrass pastures.

The library offers a quiet place to read, with heavy silk damask curtains and an antique Bakshaish carpet. A pair of late-eighteenth-century French porcelain lamps sit on nineteenth-century Chinese tables finished in blue lacquer.

A collection of Kentucky-born artist Henry Faulkner's paintings line the magenta walls of a guestroom. Eighteenth-century French chairs flanking a seventeenth-century English console introduce a more traditional note.

Overleaf
A soft pastel palette in the drawing room creates an elegant setting for the painting collection, which includes works by de Chirico and Cezanne as well as sporting paintings by Philipp Ferdinand de Hamilton and Alfred de Dreux. The furnishings are predominantly Italian and French.

A covered bridge across a stream and a sinuous dry-laid stone wall are features of the rolling landscape.

ALEXANDER MOORE HOUSE

LEXINGTON

1836

METICULOUSLY PRESERVED, TWO SHORT BLOCKS from the center of Lexington, is Gratz Park occupying a tract of land established in 1781 by order of the Virginia Assembly—Kentucky was part of Virginia until 1792. Ringed with fine examples of a variety of architectural styles dating from the 1790s to the 1970s, it was the city's first locally designated historic district and placed on the National Register of Historic Places in 1973. In the words of Lexington's architectural historian, the late Clay Lancaster, "The park has charm, atmosphere, a sense of tranquility and of history, and it provides an oasis of planting tucked into the cityscape."

Named after Benjamin Gratz, a leading hemp manufacturer and trustee of Transylvania University, which occupied space there from its founding in 1793, until it was burned down and forced to move in 1829, the park was a favorite venue for horse shows, band concerts, and public meetings. Sometimes locked by Gratz to keep out the public, it was deeded to the city in the mid-twentieth century and today is open to all.

One of the most architecturally intact buildings in the park is the Alexander Moore House. Built in 1836 by Moore, who ran a stationery store in town and sold the first school books to the city, the Federal townhouse is distinguished by a Flemish bond pattern in the blue-painted brick facade, window frames and shutters, and a copper roof. Next door in the garden of the Peter Paul House is an enormous gingko tree said to have been planted by Henry Clay.

Topped with a copper roof, and sheathed in bricks arranged in a Flemish bond pattern, the Federal-style townhouse dating from the 1830s is home to an outstanding contemporary art collection.

Preceding pages
A self-portrait by Stephan Balkenhol takes center stage in the living room. Above the fireplace are Dennis Oppenheim's stag heads, made with antlers that light up.

Above
In the master bedroom, contemporary art, including a series of photographs by Louisville artist Steven Hull of "local characters," combines with a family collection of Persian rugs.

Opposite
Contemporary art is juxtaposed with the classical detailing of the dining room mantel.

An acknowledged architecture and history buff, the current owner previously lived in another house in Gratz Park, so he felt fortunate to be able to buy the Moore house in 1996. Influenced by the Shakers, who had a large community in the nearby town of Pleasant Hill, Moore had created a minimalist interior with little ornamentation, making it easy for the current owner to create a gallery-like space for his collection of contemporary art. "Contemporary art can really announce itself in an older, simpler space," he says. "And art collecting is a little like the horse business, based on research, provenance, and history. It's as challenging to identify emerging artists and predict the course of their careers as it is to select a good horse, hoping for success and a productive breeding or racing career."

The modest building accommodates a dining and living room, the master bedroom suite, a guestroom, library, a sunroom with French doors opening to the outside, and a "travelers' room"—an old-fashioned term from the 1800s for rooms positioned over the kitchens, which were separate structures at the time. The doorway and stoop are later additions. In the back is a pocket garden laid out by local landscape designer Bill Henkel and graced by magnolia, boxwood, hydrangea, hornbeams, and sycamores.

Above
Brightened with a shag rug from the 1960s, the guest room features paintings by Alfred Jensen on the left and by Japanese artist Yoyoi Kusama above the bureau.

Opposite
The travelers' room is furnished with a leather Eames chair, and pillow-cozy sofa. A painting by Vietnamese artist Dinh Q. Lê is at the right.

The spacious dining room is centered with a custom Shaker-style, table surrounded by Philippe Starck's Lucite chairs. The crystal chandelier was found on eBay.

JANUARY HOUSE

LEXINGTON

C. 1810, EXPANDED 1846

MOST LOCALS STILL refer to this house as January House, after the man who built the original brick structure, consisting of a two-story main section flanked by two symmetrical wings, around 1818. When Thomas January, a hemp manufacturer, died in 1825, the house served first as a school and then as the Episcopal Theological Seminary before being bought by Tobias Gibson in 1846.

Gibson was a wealthy Louisiana sugar planter whose father had been a free man of color (a fact that was long a family secret) and whose son, Randall Lee Gibson, became a U.S. Senator from Louisiana as well as one of the founders of Tulane University. Gibson attended college in Lexington and married a local girl, the aptly named Louisiana Breckenridge Hart. When the couple bought January Hall as a summer home, they commissioned architect Thomas Lewinski to add grandeur in the form of a monumental portico with fluted Ionic columns and wide front steps. Two years later, John McMurtry was hired to raise the height of the wings to two full stories. He also added four new bedrooms as well as one of Lexington's first bathrooms on the second floor. On the first floor, an enormous reception hall was created when the wall between the two west reception rooms was removed and replaced with a screen of Ionic columns. All of the first floor public rooms still bear the marks of Gibson's Louisiana roots in the form of elaborate plaster ceiling medallions, marble mantels, and imposing gilt mirrors with matching window valances that were shipped up from New Orleans.

The Ionic columns and ironwork were added to the front of the January House in the 1840s when the house was greatly enlarged.

Preceding Spread
The grandeur of the double parlor is achieved by the gilt mirrors, valances, marble mantels, plaster moldings, and columns that have been a part of the house since the mid-nineteenth-century renovation.

The double parlor, which is locally known as The Ballroom, has hosted hundreds for events and dances. The furniture is a mix of pieces John Wilkirson has inherited from his family or acquired from his antiques shops. The colorful mural, painted by Wilkirson, extends over the walls and is visible in the various mirrors throughout the space.

The current owner, antiques dealer John Wilkirson, is slowly undoing the damage of the generations since the Civil War when Gibson lost the house. He has removed "dropped in" bathrooms and closets, as well as the dropped ceiling and dark beams in the dining room. By painstakingly scraping away the paint on the massive doors of the public rooms, he has uncovered the original faux graining, and he is painting his own "abstracted landscape" murals on the walls of the reception hall. The house, he says, was a "coup de foudre." Fortunately, given the state of his surroundings, he is a patient lover. When one of the plaster medallions fell from the ceiling, he simply arranged the pieces on the table below as an art installation of sorts. One day, he says, he'll have it reconstructed: "I love a project."

Above
Hanging over the front-hall mantel is a portrait of Charlotte Hart Price, an ancestor of Wilkirson's and a member of an old Lexington family.

Opposite
When the Gibson family occupied January House, all the bedrooms were located upstairs. Today, this bedroom occupies the old dining room. The trunks by the bed are old 1920s hatboxes repurposed as a miniature stairway for Wilkirson's dog.

The library and study features paintings by friends and found artworks. A family portrait set over a gilt mirror hangs over the fireplace.

Preceding page, right
The dining room is in the oldest section of the house. Antique family silver sits on the sideboard.

Preceding page, left
The kitchen, once the sunroom, stretches along the back of the ballroom and dining room. An antique wooden extension ladder is suspended from the ceiling displaying a collection of woven baskets.

GAINESWAY FARM

LEXINGTON

1965

LOCATED ON SOME OF THE FINEST LAND in the Golden Crescent of the Inner Bluegrass region of Kentucky, Gainesway Farm was established in 1965 by John R. Gaines, the man behind the creation of the Breeders' Cup. Graham Beck purchased Gainesway Farm in 1989 and subsequently acquired the adjoining C. V. Whitney and Greentree Farms. The 1,500 fertile acres that make up Gainesway have produced, and will continue to produce, an impressive roster of champions and legendary names.

Antony Beck took over the leadership of Gainesway after his father retired. He and his wife, Angela, and their five children live on the farm in a house designed by Louisville architect Dan Preston in 1996 and modeled after a historic Lexington tobacco farm of the 1830s.

Gainesway sits in the rolling landscape of Bluegrass Country.

Situated among magnificent old-growth trees with a collection of rare oaks that encompasses more than seventy species, including a Valley oak and an Oglethorpe oak, and a plethora of gardens, the farm was designated an arboretum by the American Public Garden Association in 1998, the first horse farm to be so honored.

Gardens are Beck's passion. Working with garden designer David Hruska, he has created dozens of them, each with its own theme. They include a boxwood herb garden, *potager* or kitchen garden, a fleur-de-lys garden with four water features, an apple orchard, and a winter garden of evergreens. The *potager*, with a decorative pear espalier and lily-and-snapdragon border, is one of the last projects completed by British garden designer Rosemary Verey. There is also greenhouse, which is used to overwinter vegetables, trees and flowers.

One of the historic barns.

Above
Guesthouse.

Opposite
One of the four circle barns.

Also on the property are a stone-and-clapboard house that holds the farm's office and a guesthouse built by the Whitneys in the 1930s. Tragically, the guesthouse burned down in the 1950s, but Mr. Whitney had it rebuilt to identical specifications. Beck bought the house from Mrs. Whitney and has used it to host guests from throughout the world.

Barns abound—for foals, yearlings, and stallions. The stallion complex, with eight barns, features landscaping and layout by the noted designer A. E. Bye, whose penchant for features depending on changes in season or the light of day was exemplified by a 450-foot serpentine wall built of local stone that disappeared when viewed from the main house. The complex itself, designed by architect Theodore Ceraldi, was honored by an award from American Institute of Architects in 1984. Also unique are the four circle barns, a form originally built to hold show cattle and breeding stock and now used for horses.

The walled garden with the orchard beyond.

243

Iroquois Hunt Club

LEXINGTON

1880

ACKNOWLEDGMENTS

First and foremost I would like to thank my son, Elio, for his patience and good humor throughout this project. I am also very grateful to my dad, Carl, for initiating my interest in historic properties by taking me to visit wonderful places in England and France when I was young.

This book would not exist without the initial idea of my friend Antony Beck and the generosity of his whole family—the highlight of my visits being spending time with Lily.

Gay Reading was instrumental in selecting the properties to feature based on his deep knowledge of the region and its history, evident as well in his introduction to the book.

I learned so much from Elizabeth White at the Monacelli Press, who paved the way and orchestrated the process of publication. Thanks to Michael Vagnetti and Patrick Seymour for their design and production work.

Tommy Agriodimas is a genius. Period.

The support I received from Melody Brynner, Jordan Shippenberg, Danielle Barkoski, Kelly Charles, and Troy Singh at Art-Department was immeasureable.

Ken Kobayashi at TREC made everything sunny . . . even when it wasn't.

Thanks to Dave Todd for assisting on the shoots and to Jeff Hylton for piloting the helicopter.

And special thanks to Phillip Bloch and Tanya Minhas for their friendship and support.

Finally, I would like to acknowledge the owners and stewards of the houses included in the book, who have all been exceptionally supportive of the project and generous with their time and knowledge: John Wilkirson, Kitty Graddy Tonkin, John Carloftis, the Simpson family, Lucy Hamilton and Matthew Carter, Marylou Whitney and John Hendrickson, Meg Jewett, Jim and Martha Birchfield, Eric Brooks at Ashland, Karla Nicholson at Liberty Hall, David Stuart at Ward Hall, Ron Bryant at Waveland, Jerry Miller and Lilla Mason at Iroquois, Amy Gundrum at the Headley Whitney Museum, and the staff at the Shaker Village at Pleasant Hill.